BLUE HANUMAN

ALSO BY JOAN LARKIN

For Kate,
with deepest
admiration
+ affection,
Joan

BLUE HANUMAN

Joan Larkin

Hanging Loose Press
Brooklyn, New York

Published by Hanging Loose Press, 231 Wyckoff Street, Brooklyn, New York 11217-2208. All rights reserved. No part of this book may be reproduced without the publisher's written permission, except for brief quotations in reviews.

www.hangingloosepress.com

Printed in the United States of America
10 9 8 7 6 5 4 3 2 1

Cover art: *Hanuman Revealing Rama and Sita in His Heart*, watercolor on paper, 18 x 11, mid-19th to early 20th century, West Bengal, India, artist unknown. Museum purchase, Peabody Essex Museum, Salem, Massachusetts.

Cover design: Marie Carter

ISBN 978-1-934909-38-6

Library of Congress cataologing-in-publication available on request.

For Eileen Myles

CONTENTS

I

IN YOUR SIDE-RAILED BED, FACES

EYE OF NEWT

I was larval. I dreamed myself
downstairs in pj's, still in my coma.
Bach, he said, and I lay next to the radio.
Dark amber spread through my girl-brain.
Eye of newt already nestled there, an egg
glued to a twig. My pale, bespectacled brother
set me on a leaf and watched me fatten.
Franz Kafka, he said, and my new, long feelers
brushed the wall. Girl Before a Mirror
was tacked there, torn from *Life*,
her twin pear-belly worm pink
as my own. Half curled, half crawling,
I burst through skin after skin. *Art*, I said,
and my wings fanned slowly open.

PHOTO

Everyone in it dead now—Dad,
three, in a skirt—and I see her

again, the unnamed woman. She
is me. No one to introduce us:

Hello, Me. Unruly eyebrow woman,
eyes sepia but blue—they must be;

hair pulled slant, frame bent
lensward, skeptical mouth

smiling—I know you. How did you
leash your mind, when you looked through

the window over the sink
or stared through water

at your veined hand?

IN YOUR SIDE-RAILED BED, FACES

brushed late nights on paper,
mouth-knots, dark inkwash eyes

staring into the abyss.
World taped to the wall

of your next-to-last room.
After they moved you, no

more making. Your face swollen
and no sign you saw me

wearing the fright mask.
Grief, or my face under it.

TROUGH

Long block, black stone,
the brimming slab—
bitter red and copper
seep into us
and into us the small
notebook in his coat,
still undissolved poems
in bread-bought pencil
fused to each other
with blood and body fluids
in soaked dirt of a mass grave

In memory of Miklós Radnóti, 1909-1944

14

BLUE HANUMAN

A four-armed flutist took me
to the blue avatar: stone blue
monkey, whiskers silver,
broken beads silver—paint
dashed by the artist on cheap paper.
Bought for a few annas, God
kneels, looks left. Intense concentration.
His ink hands rip open his chest,
pull skin aside like a velvet curtain—
Rama and Sita alive at his core.
And what devotion shall my flesh
show, and my broken-open breast?
His blueblack tail flicks upward,
its dark tip a paintbrush loaded blue.

eye

some of my
legs swim some
eat what blooms
between ice crystals
in lightless brine

i'm resting my
no-weight on
your steel cable

your camera
six hundred feet
under the ice shelf
measures my eye
staring at you

ARTEMISIA

In her third painting of Judith, a velvet knot
of arms, head, fists. He's

draped in carmine folds. Her gown is gold.
She's forced his sword into his dense neck.

Under him, the deep crease between mattresses:
a blood-soaked vagina.

SQUARE OF BEVELED GLASS

Hag—first thought.
I can't be tender.

On my left face, in bathroom light,
a climbing-rope of flesh, next

to a seam. Its knife-sharp sister
cut in clay on the right. The two

bracket a frown. Beads edge
my scalp—more rope inside the skin.

Eyes deep, under dark smears.
Tongue thrust out, a gargoyle joke.

Don't wag that sick thing.
For once, I can't see

regrets night tosses up.
Only a face-shaped question mark.

STUDIES FOR A CRUCIFIXION

after Francis Bacon

Oil smeared with dust
to last: lush rage-orange.

Meat splayed on a table.
The business-suited, rubber-

suited stare elsewhere.
Black windows gape.

Meat hangs from lucite,
thick green line touching.

Centered: meat odalisque
on smeared bed. Meat-nothing—

THE PORCH

I saw a moth twisting on a stalk,
rapt with sucking, and knelt to watch.
It was a curled leaf—wormholes
and rust, hung by a fine hair,
and I was alive then, hungry and filled.
Fog thinned and light caught silk,
a bridge from porch rail to blown rose
to the web specked with gold bodies.
And out of her small, steel body,
the maker kept forming her shining dome.

BAT IN THE PARLOR

Silhouette torn from the Eocene,
black leaf flickering at the edge,
scything the air—nothing
to reap midflight for your
wings' carryall, you catch
the curtain with clawed thumbs.
Dark comma, what door
did you come through? All I know
comes from those who sealed your eyes
to see how you hunt blind, who tied
your jaws and sealed your mouth
to watch you blunder into their wires.
Just now you made some swift circuits
and left. I never saw you go.

FRONTISPIECE

Her face facing the lens
a moonstone set with shadows

or glowing moon itself.
Movement-in-stillness,

her lungs under silk
opcn and close.

A mind turned inside out.
Silver, light-exposed,

washed in mercury, salt-fixed, sealed
in glass evacuated of air.

She broke the first glass and kept
launching   Some flew ten feet

Each explosion wanted the next
and when she'd nothing left to throw

kitchen covered in shards   floor
shining   hands stinging   shard

sticking out of one cheek   she stood
in what she'd made   and was satisfied

LEGS TIPPED WITH SMALL CLAWS

When the lake trembles,
hairs on her legs and feet
can tell a fish from a leaf
and calculate
how far to lunge—

legs the same silver
as weathered wood
and striped like medieval
Sienese columns,
green-black alternating
with lighter hairs.

Sometimes it's her mate
she liquefies to drink him inside out,
then cleans each of her velvet legs,
scraping them on her fangs,
wiping them across her eyes.

Her wetsuit is a film of trapped air
like burnished silver.
She floats up dry to the surface.
Her legs wait, listening.

II

SING TO ME

THE COMBO

In barlight alchemized: gold pate, the bellmouth
tenor, liquor trapped in a glass. The E-flat
clarinet chases time, strings shudder,
remembering the hundred tongues. Here comes old
snakeshine, scrolls stored in the well, here comes
the sobbing chazzan. O my lucky uncle,
you've escaped the czar's army. Thunder
is sweet. Here comes the boink, boink bossa
nova slant of light. Snow-dollars
dissolve on a satin tongue. The river
swells green, concrete trembles, and we
sweat, leaning toward mikes and wires
as the last tune burns down to embers. Ash-
whispers. We were born before we were born.

SING TO ME

Chipped ivory,
wire into the wall,
a hole for headphones—

this piano came from that one,
the first piano, a dark wooden
body we sheltered in, a father
broad as an ark. I could float

alone in it, go back and forth,
E-flat, E, and slip between
tipped sky and dirty-penny
taste in the throat, not-Joan.

When his hands came down
and his voice drew us
into the floating house,
loud ungainly chords
shined a way home.

When a voice rests,
the room goes on ringing.
His timbre made the shape of my life.
Where they took him, was there a piano?

This one, electric, gold,
I think is my little mother
back from darkness.
I'll press the keys.
Sing to me, and I'll know.

WEDDELL SEAL

I fell from sealmother's
liquid womb onto fast-ice
and she suckled me with her thick
milk and kept me, fifty days.
We lived in the wind.
Under the ice in no-light
trills, buzzes, thumps
filled the water and rang in my body.
I scraped breathing holes with my teeth,
held my breath, slowed my blood,
sank deep, breathed out
bubbles to flush the icy fish;
devoured silverfish, squid, octopus,
giant toothfish, bald notothen.
A male bit my neck and gripped me.
A cub curled inside me. I bore
many cubs and let them suck. Left them
when the time came. My teeth
worn to nubs, skua will make
quick food of me when I starve
above the ice. Or if my carcass
drops to the sea floor, red
sea stars, worms, and flesh-eating
amphipods will slowly cover
me and devour my meat.
I'm standing in wind,
seal flesh still warm.

INUIT LITHOGRAPH

Owl with a twenty-seven-feather headdress
plays a squeezebox hung from a neckstrap.
Her beak, black wedge on snow, owl smile,
arrow, points to the red accordion. She
could be singing to a lemming
she'll flay with her talons. Her maker
etched a hundred curved wingfeathers,
as many again to fleck her breast, her face,
feet feathered for Arctic wind. Her blood-
red concertina, row of pearl buttons,
sits where my owl lungs would open and close
if I were owl. Sting, snow.
Sing, death screeching

TRANSIT

Some of us leaned in hard and closed our eyes.
Some were plugged into headphones. One was hunched,
mouth on his fist like Rodin's Thinker. All of us somber
and separate, though one rested on her lover's shoulder,
staring into the void. We breathed refrigerated air
as the metal snake forced itself through the tunnel,
hissing, screeching, opening and closing with a sigh.
Then the humming began: the four men heaved forward
cleaving our silence, smiling, swaying. Stand By Me
or The Lion Sleeps it didn't matter. Their close notes
said there were bees and water and blown glass
even in this yellow-lit raft of sweat and fear.
I didn't mind when they praised Jesus. They held out their paper bag,
and some of us looked, and two or three dropped in a dollar.

AT THE GATE

Miz Pearsons, guardian of the two doors
to Holy Ghost Pentecostal, was dark gold
and round as Krishna's globe of stolen butter.
Her bee's eyes knew the predators. *You*
gotta wait, to the jittery dude outside
who wanted a prayer. She led me down a damp hall
to what I lusted for. *Next he's gonna want*
what's in the basket.

                  The piano stood, as in the photo,
on cracked linoleum. One key was chipped—
I'd learn its flaws. But first she wanted me to know
I'm out here every day, but His blood covers me.

GONE

I checked the seconds as they fell
from the flat face on my wrist
into Nothing. Pressed my ear
against the metallic click.
Wristwatch, make me rich.

I passed a man on a box
holding a waxed cup.
Fifties in my purse, I glanced
sideways and muttered something.
He wished me well as I passed.

Francis sang in the wind:
  Sickness, heal me.
  Rags, dress me.
  Time, be silent.
  Beggar, bless me.

IN GOLD LEAF ON A HINGED PANEL

She stands on nothingness almost,
on a stone blue cloud—
winged imago, intersex angel,
no breasts, no outthrust larynx,
old-young eyes tilted. A tooled halo.
No shadow, seam, or sumptuary law
in heaven. Knife-thin wings
lie flat behind a blood gown,
cinnabar of streaked sunset and pulsing
wound, lavish folds and bands.
Cloak scrolled like a C clef,
recap of red hoop—
the moonround tambourine
those fingers tap, gently
as you'd hold an egg. Gold
disks shiver. The hand echoes
a hand that held a brush as prayer,
no line ever changed or retouched.
They say he wept when he painted a crucifixion.

CELL

A fly was observing The Great Silence,
cakewalking six-legged across the pane.
Slow, slow. My first thought was to kill,
but couldn't. Not in Francis's room.
I watched her
rub thin wires together as she crossed
and recrossed. Milk light
shone through her veined wings.
One of her kind, corpse akimbo,
lay on the sill, wings primly folded.
I slid the window open, but she
kept treading glass Braille,
obeying her hidden law:
>Turn in a circle, fly
>to the bottom of the frame, crawl
>between glass and gray felt.
>Then make a sudden exit
on a cold current, out over bare oaks.
River and sky were mute,
and I was a fool and happy.

UPCOUNTRY

Baby owlet, purple owlet—I keep singing,
Road. Where are you riding me? What's
this little Bavaria deep in woods, men
standing round with beers? Those leaves
just shivered; keep rolling, little Silver.
It's real woods now—no Sof-Serv, no Satan,
no Olde Flea Motel. Those are vultures
perched in that oak, six-foot wingspread, eyes
fixed on the deer's corpse. I don't grudge
their blood-filled feast. If we reach Red Hill, reach
the mouse kitchen, I'll tear through tomato flesh,
I'll kill the loaf. No moon, Road. Don't quit me now.
I want to sleep in the mouse house, I want to watch
from the porch while a doe tears leaves with her teeth.

THREE-PART INVENTION

I followed the ambulance hell to hell.
Her words stung, but I leaned in
close to the buzzing strings.

*

Who sees a woman whole, even when she sings
an old, dirty song in a metal bed?
When earth gapes for her.

*

But then a girl's rage tore me
and I saw soft globes inside
coated with gold jelly—trembling, Mother.

CORRIDOR

Did Dad call her *Dollface?*
What does come back:
how she lay all night and morning
on her back, gurney locked
under dirty light. Still
back in her brother's fever:
The baby's screaming.
How once, her eyes flew open,
saw me.
Now I'm locked in that event horizon—
no light no time
but what I dream she saw.
Dollface. This
costly bolted seat
trembles as I hurtle toward a kind of home.

I DREAM OF GINSBERG'S MOROCCAN FOOTSTOOL

Skin inked with fire
and sewn: his low table.
Bowed, skullcapped, Allen
touches a tattered handle.
This is my ear.
Hawk-faced man
hacks off the soft fold:
Now take your ear.
And you took it in both
hands, staring
into the burning-place.
Then sang.

III

ON THE MOON

Before I saw him
I felt his blind cane digging
for purchase in my chest. I
was the road. Rocks, gnarled roots,
sudden hissing. I was the town
on the mountain, not drug sleep
in a fifth-floor walkup. What was death
to him? He had force I couldn't argue,
pressed the cane stubborn into my chest.
Then I saw him: screen door open,
cancer body in thin pajamas,
snow up to his knees, smiling.

JUROR

I woke on my left side, hoping a drenched
sycamore and white sky were all I needed
to hold off morning, that the only mouths
were birds, obbligato over whining engines.
Thick snakes of rain slid down the cheap façade
and darkened a raw stump, all that was left
of a young, sick tree. I wanted someone to blame
for scars and hacked-off branches and the lie
of seven flowerings. Fumes from a trash bag
stung me. Light was knifing through a cloud
and would be ruthless. In the tangled yard,
I saw a ragged weed globed with clear drops
only a hair could hold. Then it was time.
Downtown, they lined us up and walked us in.

RUSTED SAAB, ROUTE 1

Noon, and no one can fix *nothin'*
till Monday. If my grave on wheels
gets there, will you still be there, cur-
ator of your dust museum, your *Physics*
of Music, your stooped back, your twisting
catacombs of *I wish*. I wish
to listen to your oldest joke. So smile,
Brother, show me your teeth. Say *Maybe*.

ON THE MOON

He walked so slow I had time to pick
splinters of granite from the dirt.
The dog was nosing weeds at the verge.
A clump hung from her tail, hardened earth
caught in a snarl of fur I wanted to cut.
To bathe her, too, if he'd had a tub or a hose.
No-see-ums stung my face, my bare neck,
and I worried the bites as we walked,
this time only a tenth of a mile till he leaned
on the knobby cane Ann gave him
before her catastrophe. *I'd better turn back now.*
Brother, I turned with you. I sat
in the house where grief settles
into the dust. I touched my souvenir stone.

KNOT

Who came to stop the two men
for they must have stopped

nights ago on an uptown sidewalk
knot of flesh

center of a gawking crowd
One flung his body

on the other   muttering murder
struck the curb

the other clung like a lover
Whose red-dark face

arm locked on neck
pavement tearing through cloth

body knotted to body
Not-god   pry me apart

THE SENTENCE

If I were there, I'd wait with the women
indoors by law. I'd think of sun
heating the men's faces, listen
for the girl's high-pitched love confession,
watch lips through a glistening beard
read out the sentence. Silence, then cheers,
screams, a kind of soccer match.
I'd see the girl, shrouded, faceless
in our common garment, I'd study
the crowd for her flushed brother
soaked through his shirt, sun high
for the half hour it takes to kill
the girl. Then the bound man.
I hear exultant yells as the two
bodies are rolled face down in their blood.
I'm shaping dough, smearing egg.
When the men are tired, I serve them, I wait
while they drink, eat, empty themselves
then sleep.

FLESH

Hooves were forbidden, but she fed us
stringy liver, thick tongue, gray kishkes
crammed with something soft. She had a bulb
of garlic, a handful of salt, some wretched carrots.
Drew out blood with salt, clamped her grinder
and fed chunks into it and forced them down.
She let me turn the crank, and red worms
fell to the bowl. I ate according to the Law
and the cow's flesh became my flesh.
Now I lower my head to eat, moan when I wake
from the fear dream, the one where we shove
one another down the ramp toward the violent
stench and the boy's knife. He lifts his arm
in a rhythm I've always known.

CHICKEN

Who twisted her neck,
scorched her pinfeathers,

slung her in slow
circles around the head

to be rid of sin—
and who made sin—

Mister God
in his stained apron,

tight suit, hat out of time,
birdshit in the crease of his shoe.

Who kept her till the day,
salted her, bled her,

dumped her on a truck,
let poor eat poor,

can't look me in the eye
and not think *filthy hole*,

for I'm a dirty bird no
wire cage can save.

MONKEY DREAM

The baby's fastened to his mother's stomach
chewing seeds, high up in liquid heat. Blow darts
in hollowed shafts of cane make the best monkey hunting,
so quiet you can drop two or three before they hear.
The meat's tough as rubber and smells like rot.
It's hard stripping off their fur with a knife,
piling them pink and naked, set to boil. Some nights
in green hell there's nothing to eat but a bowl of thin
monkey broth. Some nights Cook howls in his sleep
as they come toward him whinnying, raising their knife.

DOLL COLLECTOR

A box—boxes
lined up each the same,
cellophane taut
over the tame female.
Wide eyes, sprayed-on shoes
all I remember. And you,
master of these shelves,
I want to label and keep you
where I last knew you,
your stone handshake,
your glare, your *Goodbye Joan*.

MOURNING FRAGMENT

Suri danced in the women's bar,
rebbe's permission unasked. Danced
the day the temple burned. Light
in that room almost a solid, she moved
too slow for her strange thoughts,
pressed to a woman. Told me this
in the bookstore café where she wrote,
sons in school, notebooks spilling
from her full bag, nothing finished.
Her mother survives her, friends
surround her table. None tell
of her dancing but mourn her *lost
pages*—and even this fragment
you must doubt.

THE BOOT

The boot is born
in a molding machine
and a girl in a mask
breathes fumes, presses the pedal
fast as is in her power
and the boot takes dominion.
What does she dream, nothing

on two legs, machine
stamping her mouth, eye, ovary,
pushing out boot after boot.
I wore her, I was her,
I dragged the boot uphill
past the museum to the shul,
the chuppah on cracked pavement,

and the girl circles a scraggly beard
seven times while a dead
rebbe's recorded voice blesses
us warns us, tape hissing as if
where he is it's raining or 1943,
as if a corpse can be made whole
by children pushing out more
children.

PRESCRIPTION

You sent me a recipe for healing:
no mushrooms, fruit, nothing fermented, no
yeast, no cheese, no honey, nothing sweet
that in the dank lab of my cells
would heat and swell. *Don't
tell me you don't want to get well.*
All that stood between me and my cage
of habits, my dragged chain of animal fear—
her dry, tight handclasp on a Paris street,
his bearish dancing that once shook my floor,
the wide open mouth of another's hunger—
between flesh and its transubstantiation
to a clear alkaline non-attachment
was—

LAKE

I split the sky-mirror,
lifting it on my blade,
and troubled the long grass
streaming beneath; I cried
to a gold bull's-eye lily's
redstained throat—hello,
twisted silver balsam—
and swore a blood-bright
cardinal flower was the flag
for a boulder matted with lichen,
cleft stone the ice sheet
lifted and heaved in her wake.
Silt and minerals washed
from the jutting slopes, up-
thrust from an ancient seabed,
same rock as the moon,
same salt as my teeth and bones
and the arm that ached
as I kept lifting the paddle;
and even in the lethal afterword
of acid in the bowl of rain,
I loved the mergansers teaching
their chicks, and the one loon
dipping her greenblack head,
diving.

WHITE IRON BED

I woke in my own bed.
While I was gone, others
had lain here sweating
but left no imprint.
The morning air was cool,
sheets weightless. I breathed,
watched leaf shadows tremble.
Nothing reminded me of before.
Through the window, across the street,
no more graffiti. Vines dangled,
swayed on scrubbed brick.
And the iron bed—
scarred paint, brass finials—shone.
Ferrying me.

RED-EARED SLIDER

When I slid from a fallen tree
into the slow Suwannee,
the gold river closed over me.
When I slid from the fallen tree,
my shell disappeared under green algae.
There was no you, there was no me
when I slid from a fallen tree
into the slow Suwannee.

IV

FIST UNOPENED

Tongue begun,
brainbud within the bud,
fist unopened, spine
curled like a question
unannealed—what
was it? Dark clot
flushed down,
squiggle of ink
curdled in seawater,
old round stone
flung into my pond.
Sunk there.

THE COVENANT

A shtik flaysh mit tsvei eigen, I was
a piece of meat with two eyes, an animal
watching another animal. She fed,
dressed, named me, flushed my waste, scrubbed my pink
skin till it sang. The kitchen was hers, where
the iceman's tongs pincered solid blocks, cream
rose in bottles, inching up past the lip,
coal roared through a chute into the cellar.
Unsaid, invisible: the weight she carried,
cold and dense as the block
the iceman shouldered, stung through his burlap rag.
I lapped her scorn, answered her bitter call.
She needed to eat. I was her meal,
I was the nearest protein.

ESCAPEE

Narrow hall, your cheek
brushed a stiff fold of machine lace

No water ringing in the kettle
No one at the sink listening

Will yourself twist the knob

The train burst through a tunnel of leaves
to saltmarsh   tall cordgrass   blind clouds

CLOTH BAG

The bag pulls on her shoulder.
2:00 a.m.—no one sees she's
carrying a wrapped fetus
hurrying past streetlamps,
looking for a dumpster.

This was in another decade,
but the city is standing—
stained skies, harsh gutturals.
And fear—where does that go?
Mine drags my side down.

No one wanted that bag of flesh.
And no one outruns her own life,
not even a strong-jawed girl in a film
who says, *Never will we speak of this.*

RESERVOIR

She stood between blacktop
and spindly pines, suckling her fawn.
They pulsed as one body releasing
the sweet milk-tide. Eyes open,
she half turned her head.
I left her rooted to cropped grass
and fawn's satiny mouth.
Her coat had not yet turned
oakleaf dark. I left the window
rolled down, let wind come in
and the rock river and the
pitcher that once kept
filling, filling as I poured.

THE DOOR

You, too, had a mother, her swollen feet
laced into oxfords, braids wound and skewered
that day she left for the hospital and turned

at the door: *Celia, take care of the baby.*
Too late to ask if you knew *women's trouble*
was code for hysterectomy, too late
to ask how you cooled your brother's

burning and how she knew he was dead
before they told her. I too know dread
in the flesh, how you had to shut the door
to a room her screams couldn't enter.

You are inside me now, as inside you
your mother: your shame-belly born from hers,
my grief-lungs from yours, eyes of no mercy.

SUMMONS

Are you asleep
Are you mute
Are you empty now
Are you alone

Ewe-mother
shrike-mother
where did you go
frost on a stone

Soft arms and harsh mouth,
you could say I've kept them
but fold a sheet my own way.
I'd like to show you.

I'm six, feverish, you're reading to me:
white alps, your shimmering alto.
Were you awake
when your last string snapped?

I'm yeast and air in a crust
quickly swallowed.

Waking in twisted sheets, I know
how the green-smocked aide hoists you.
When time is done with me,
may there be mercy.

Ewe-mother
shrike-mother
where do you go
frost on a stone

Are you asleep
Are you mute
Are you empty now
Are you alone

HERE COMES

The mother of generations,
sackful of eggs at the end of her stomach.
She scutters away from light,
knows where her kind are hiding.
Her hatchlings harden and darken, flex leather wings
and underwings branched with veins and cross-veins.
She rears her young in cracks, in damp left by a dripping tap.
She leaves trails in the air to show where food is,
to show where her flat body is waiting.
Welcomes a suitor to her nether end, his scent
aphrodisiac, his head-twisting stylish and lusty.
She follows the sweet signal of mint and vanilla,
chews the unswept crumb,
lives on glue from the back of a stamp.
She comes from tropics in the holds of ships,
flying, sprinting, chirping, hissing.
Shaking and jostling.
She rose 400 million years ago,
has a thousand names.
Men bear her to the ends of Earth.
She is locked in Baltic amber.

FAY

Came over in steerage dressed as a boy.
Squatted over the hole. Watched the sidewise-
speeding rats. Watched her mother thumb-printing
siddur pages, sounding out letters shaped
like an eye, a shoe, a doorway, black candles.
Talked to God with fire. Was God in her home.
Smiled *You're dead to me*, smiled spilling a bowl
of scalding oatmeal on a bad child. Watched
her waxy children burn. Learned a new
tongue. Pocketed dollar tips in her black apron,
grinned at customers. Showed her gold tooth
in both tongues. Ninety years an American.

THE DRESS

Leon across the table showing me Polaroids
of his fling won't say "drag." It's a *costume* party.

Rust-black pencil dress from a bargain bin,
pearl choker hiding his Adam's apple,

he's our gaunt aunt back from the grave, her grinning
lipstick. He has her voice, too, a rasp

drawn across taut wires. He bends to his snapshot,
chortling. I've seen him dance, *yeshiva bocher*

with St. Vitus' mania, and imagine him high
on weed—his liberator, along with the Reichian

he sees weekly. In young days his face
looked split, a cubist sculpture, brow crooked,

sockets askew. Now he looks up—our long-gone
aunt!—and stares with her volcanic eyes.

ST. PETE

Lowered myself into the small bluish
pool, Palmway Apartments, and started in:
my crawl, my breaststroke. Passed women waist-
deep in chlorine-scented liquid comparing
menus, all-you-can-eat buffets, and kept
counting, two hundred, three hundred laps, kept
driving my flesh forward. I was nothing
like those women. Nor was I my mother
waiting in a plastic chair, glancing up
from *McCall's*, glossy page tinged green
by her visor. Stoic or proud of me I don't
know which. She never entered the water—
my domain—where I thrashed, maniac,
cutthroat, big fish.

ENGLISH

…whose pressed lips sucked
milk from air. Who stole
flute from bone, blood
from ocean. Touched tongue
to bristle. Dug volcanic slabs
from dirt. Lit stars.
Poured fire from the king's throat
and bowed broke-kneed
in a mute globe of held breath.
Shipped mast and rudder, sold
mama na mwana, showed
us the coiled rope, showed
the shovel. Named us un-
clean. Named the nothing.
Stalked a hooting backstreet
clarinet. Flooded trenches and let
coughing drown in a gas-cloud.
Listen—a crying hinge, a scythe,
skull dance and robot stutter—
moth mother,
star I moor in.

CUT-LEAF BEECH

Half-closed eye after eye
climbs her rough-smooth swells
like the god of breasts
I worship with my touch mouth.

Silver tree skin, robin
running on two legs,
twisted rope of wisteria
tell me my nipple

is an eye. And where I
walked in milk light
trees are feeding the dark—
cars, cars rushing where I sleep.

Eye, close,
mouth, open,
blown bird press
your shaking branch—

NOTES

Trough: Hungarian poet Miklós Radnóti was murdered on a forced march from a Nazi labor camp in Bor, Yugoslavia. His last poems, written during the march, were found when a mass grave was exhumed after the war.

Artemesia: Judith beheading Holofernes was the subject of more than one painting by the 17th-century Italian Baroque artist Artemisia Gentileschi. Gentileschi's prosecution of the painter who raped her in her father's studio has sometimes eclipsed her reputation as a major artist.

Legs Tipped with Small Claws: The subject is a fishing spider, also known as a dock spider.

Chicken: In the ritual of atonement called *shlugen kapores*, performed before Yom Kippur, a live chicken is swung overhead while prayers are chanted. The believer's sins are transferred to the chicken, which is killed and given to charity.

Monkey Dream: Killing monkeys, and the cook's dream, are described in Scott Wallace's *The Unconquered*, record of a search for uncontacted tribes in the Brazilian rain forest. The phrase "green hell" is Wallace's.

Cloth Bag: "Never will we speak of this" is quoted from *4 Months, 3 Weeks and 2 Days*, a 2007 film set in Romania in 1987 during the brutal Ceausescu regime, when abortion was a crime punishable by death.

DEDICATIONS

In Your Side-Railed Bed, Faces and *Trough* are for John Masterson.

The poem *Blue Hanuman* is for Sharon Mesmer.

The Combo is for Steve Elsen, whose music inspired it.

Sing to Me is for Nick Flynn.

Weddell Seal is for Steve Turtell.

Inuit Lithograph is for Jan Heller Levi, who gave me the picture, and for Guy Klusevic, accordion virtuoso.

In Gold Leaf on a Hinged Panel is for Johann Larkin, who sent me the picture, and for Robert Bunkin and Jenny Tango, who first showed the way to the Fra Angelicos at the Convent of San Marco in Florence.

Cell, written in St. Francis's room at Holy Cross Monastery, is for Br. Robert Magliula, OHC.

Upcountry is for Naomi Bushman and Fletcher Copp.

ACKNOWLEDGMENTS

Some of these poems have appeared in earlier versions, or are forthcoming, in *Aphros, Big Bridge, Bloom, Clockhouse Review, Connotation Press: An Online Artifact, Great River Review, Hanging Loose, H.O.W. Journal, Jewish Currents, Meadowlands Muse, Narrative Northeast, New York Quarterly, Ploughshares, Plume,* Poem-A-Day (The Academy of American Poets digital series), *Poetry International, Psychology Tomorrow, Sinister Wisdom, The Wide Shore: A Journal of Global Women's Poetry,* and *thethepoetry.com.*

Special thanks to Elizabeth Clark Wessel and Argos Books for publishing the beautiful hand-sewn chapbook *Legs Tipped with Small Claws.*

I am indebted to the Academy of American Poets and the Poetry Society of America for generous support, and to Blue Mountain Center, the Djerassi Foundation, Hawthornden Castle, and the Virginia Center for the Creative Arts, where many of these poems were written.

Deepest thanks to Jean Valentine, Anne Marie Macari, and Jan Heller Levi, for extraordinary friendship, insight, and faith in these poems.

The publishers of Hanging Loose Press are high on my list of heroes for their dedication to poets and poetry over the decades. Enormous thanks to Robert Hershon, Dick Lourie, and Mark Pawlak for their support of this book, to Donna Brook for perceptive editing, and to Marie Carter for care in helping to bring it into being.